MEL BAY'S

Hymns for Harmonica

DIATONIC • CROSS-HARP • CHROMATIC

BY PHIL DUNCAN

To my daughter, Amanda Bernell Duncan

INTRODUCTION

This book presents many arranged hymns in several different keys using various harmonicas. The Diatonic, 10 hole harmonica; the Cross-Harp (blues-style), 10 hole harmonica; and the 12 or 16 hole Chromatic harmonica will be illustrated in this book. This book will give many hours of playing pleasure to the beginner as well as the advanced performer. "Praise the Lord. . . with an instrument. . . play skillfully with a loud noise." Psalm 33:3 "I will sing a new song unto Thee, O, God: upon. . . an instrument. . . will I sing praises unto Thee." Psalm 144:9

Phil Duncan

1 2 3 4 5 6 7 8 9 0

Visit us on the Web at http://www.melbay.com — E-mail us at email@melbay.com

CONTENTS

DIATONIC

Each harmonica is designed in a certain "key". When using the harmonica in that stated "key" it is called standard or straight harmonica, such as the Key of C is for the C harmonica. This also means that the center or "home" tone is the fourth hole. The key of G is the G harmonica, the key of D is for the D harmonica, and the key of F is the F harmonica, etc. Each key requires a different harmonica. This book specifically uses C, G, D, F and B♭ harmonicas. It has been necessary at times to designate the upper octave of the standard harmonica to be played instead of the middle or lower octaves. This is due to the arrangement of tones on the 10 hole harmonica.

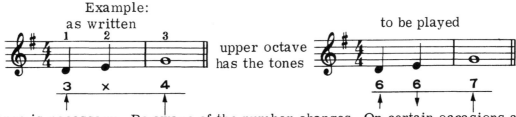

This octave change is necessary. Be aware of the number changes. On certain occasions a note will be altered to accommodate the Diatonic instrument. This note may be played in lieu of the chromatic tone.

For further information about the Diatonic harmonica see Mel Bay's DELUXE HARMONICA METHOD by Phil Duncan.

CROSS-HARP

The method for Cross-Harp is to cross over to hole 2 of the diatonic 10 hole harmonica and draw. This tone becomes the "key" tone or center and changes the "key" in which the harmonica plays. Therefore, C harp plays cross-harp in the key of G, F harp plays cross-harp in the key of C, G harp plays cross-harp in the Key of D, B flat harp plays in the key of F, etc. The cross-harp allows for half step tones not normally played on the standard or straight harmonica. Cross-Harp draw tones should begin below the pitch: **5**

This is known as "bending" the tone. Notation information:

③ = Half Step   ③ = Whole Step   ▽ = Whole step & half step

Numbers may change, but not the notes, such as an octave change.

Notes in paranthesis are subsitute notes.

For more information see: <u>BLUES HARP for Diatonic and Chromatic Harmonica</u> by Phil Duncan

CHROMATIC

This book utilizes the C Chromatic Harmonica only. The use of the slide button will give accurate half step tones on the chromatic harmonica. The 12 hole or the 16 hole chromatic harmonica is used in this book. The use of chromatic harmonica and its notation is not well established within the industry. This book will use C chromatic to express all "keys". A change of octaves (all octaves on the chromatic are the same, no missing tones, only the tones are higher or lower in pitch) becomes necessary for variety and ease of playing. EXAMPLE:

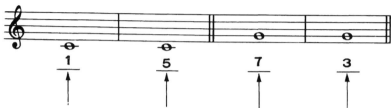

For further information see: Mel Bay's <u>CHROMATIC HARMONICA METHOD</u> by PHIL DUNCAN

GENERAL INFORMATION

1. Top arrow is the rule:

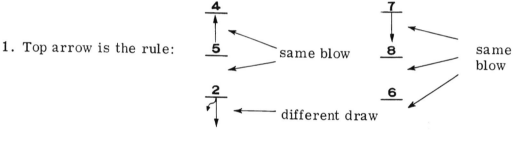

2. Length of arrow is for duration of sound: long   short

3. Tied notes: 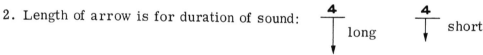 Do not repeat the second tone, but combine both durations.

. . . And I Will Dwell In The House Of The Lord Forever. Psalm 23:6

So then faith cometh by hearing, and hearing by the word of God. Romans 10:17

C harmonica, Diatonic

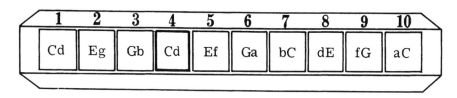

F cross - Harp

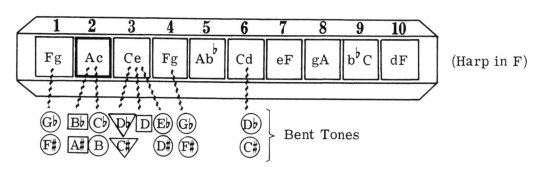

(Harp in F)

C harmonica, Chromatic

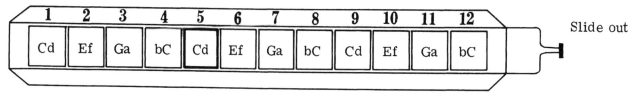

Slide out

OH, IT IS JESUS

Source Unknown

THE OLD TIME RELIGION

KEY OF C
SWEET HOUR OF PRAYER

William Walford (1772-1850)

William Bradbury (1816-1868)

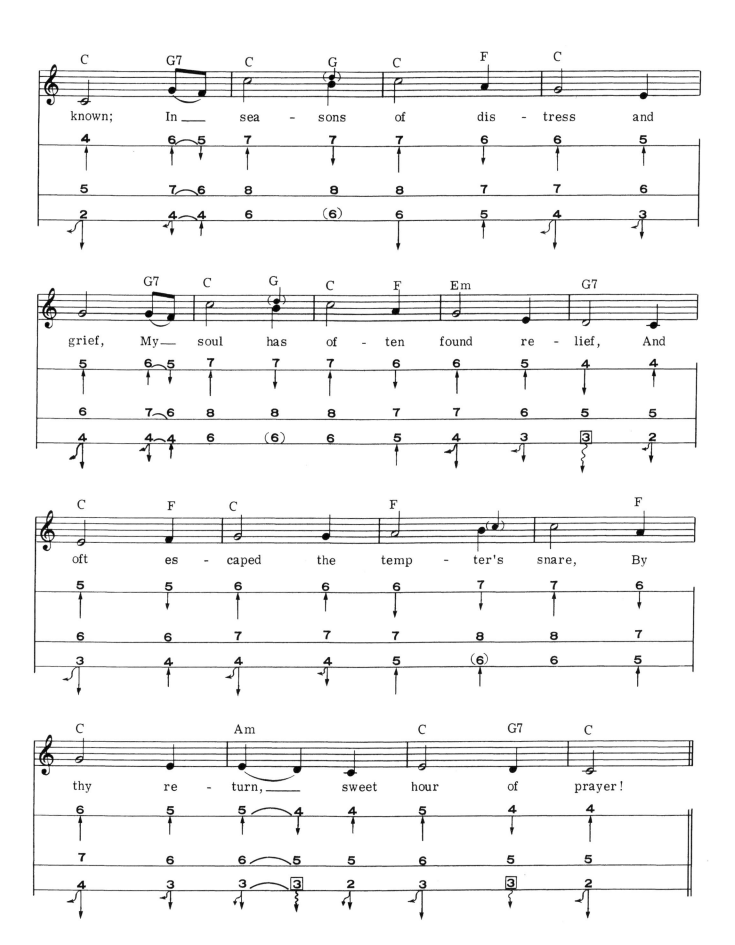

9

I LOVE HIM

Foster

THIS LITTLE LIGHT OF MINE

STOP AND LET ME TELL YOU

Source Unknown

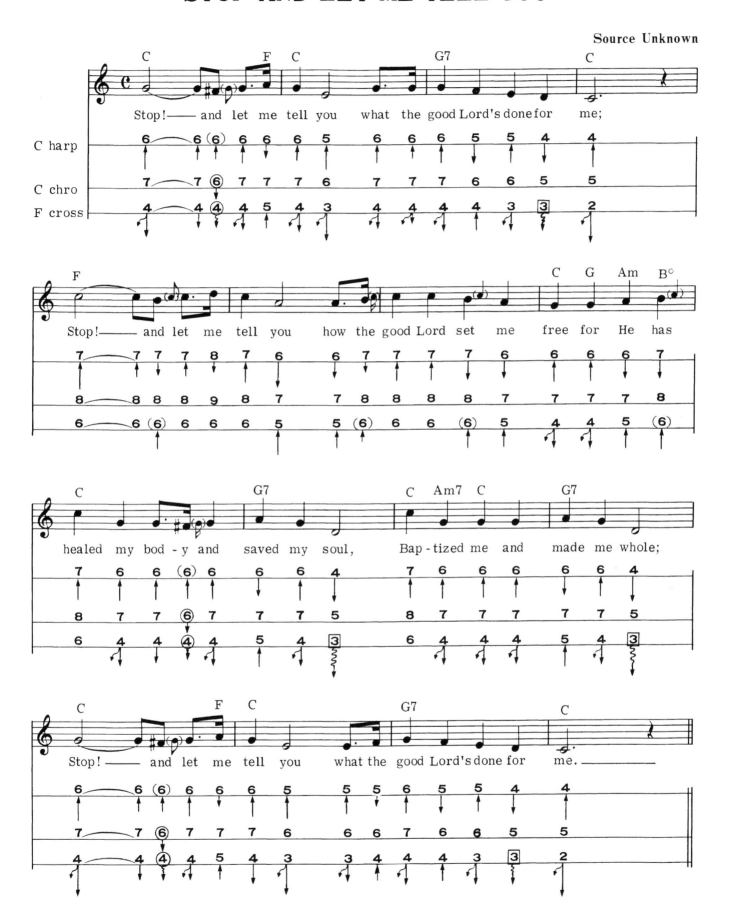

TIS BURNING IN MY SOUL

Delia T. White 19th Century

W. J. Kirkpatrick (1828-1921)

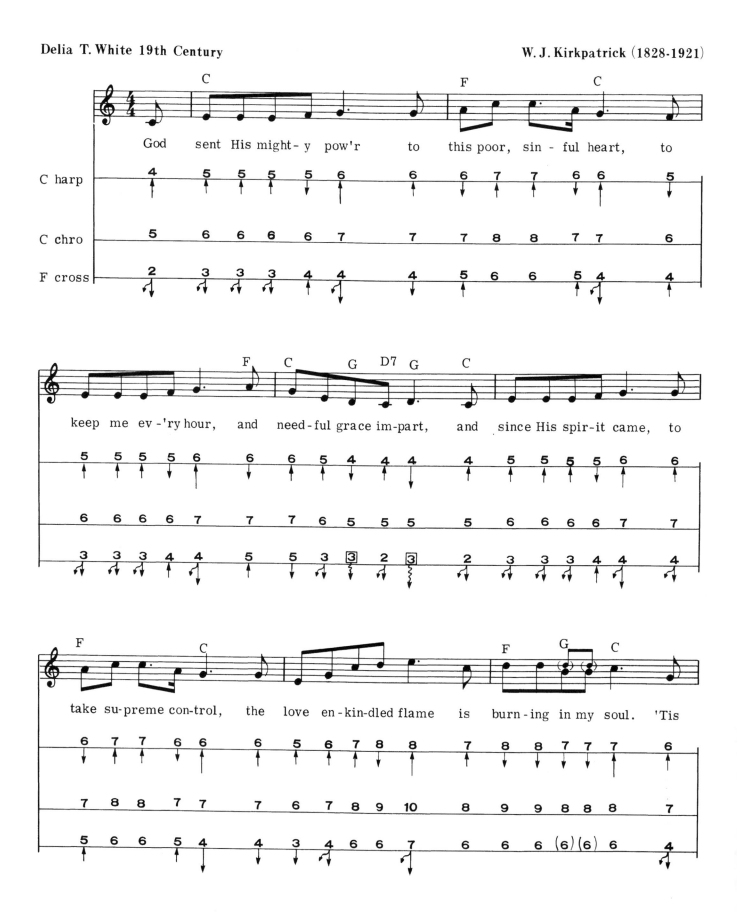

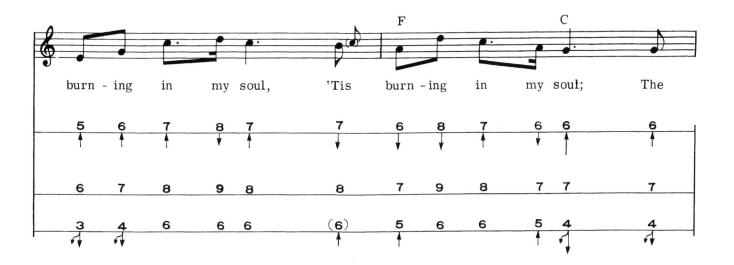

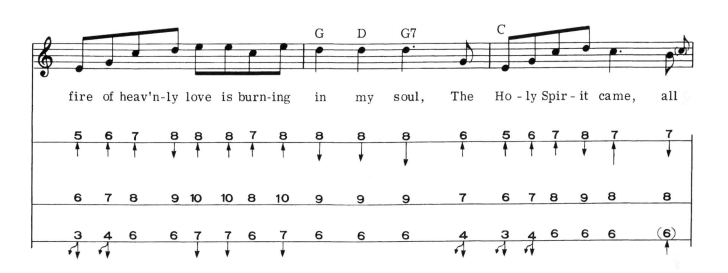

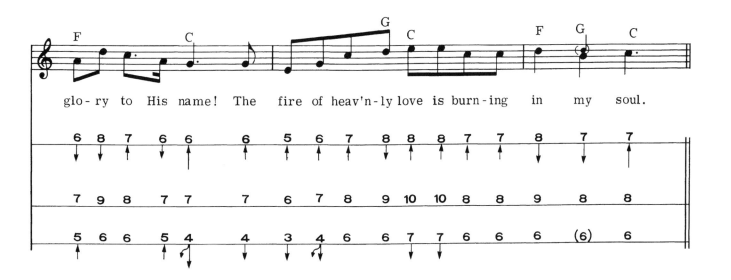

THERE IS A FOUNTAIN FILLED WITH BLOOD

W. Cowper (1800)

American Melody

NEVER ALONE

Source Unknown

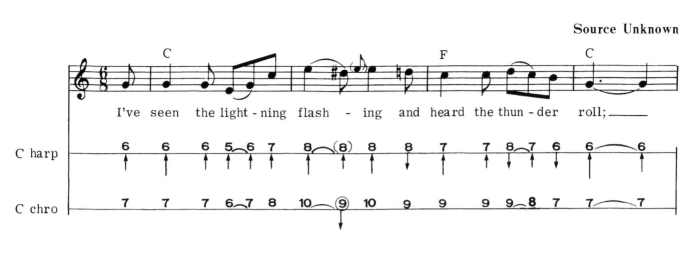

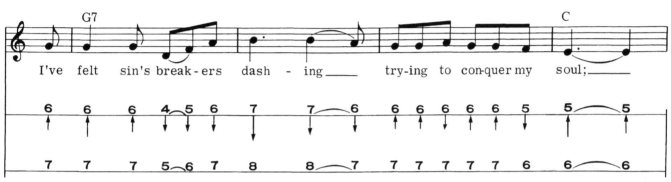

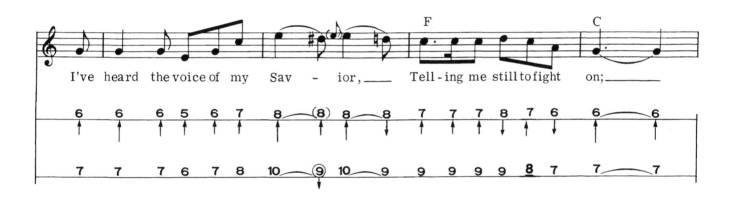

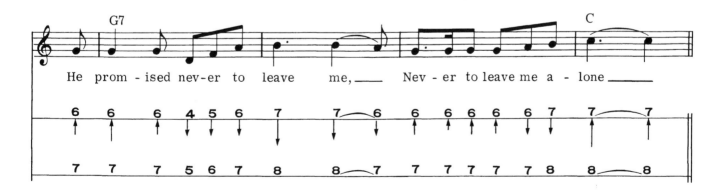

MINE EYES HAVE SEEN THE GLORY

Julia Ward Howe

William Steffe

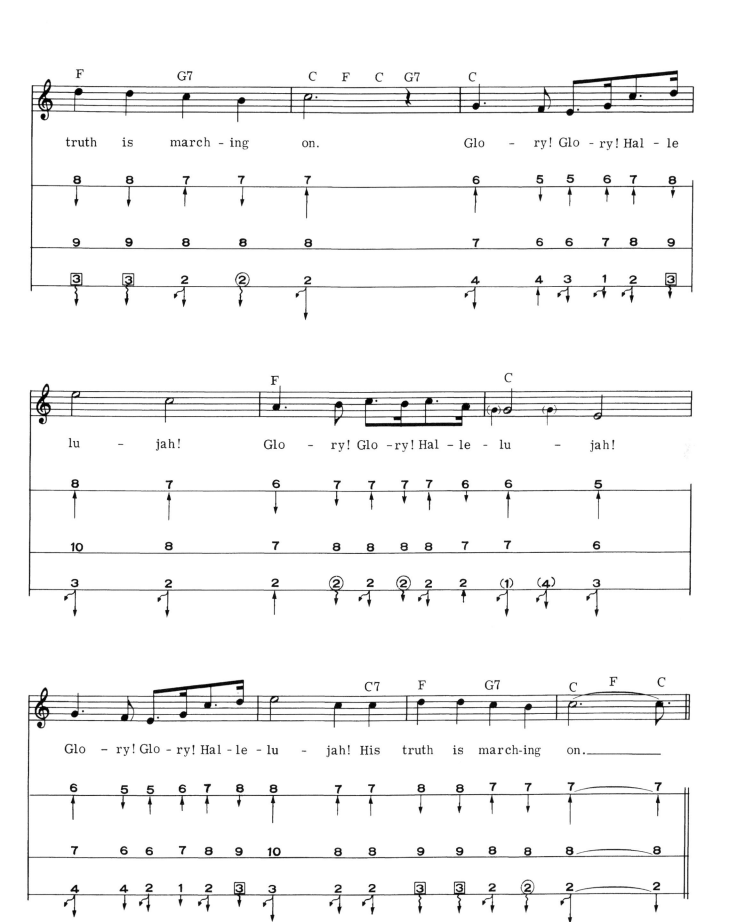

KUM BA YAH

The Lord is my strength and song. Psalm 118:14

JOSHUA FIT THE BATTLE OF JERICHO

Spiritual

19

JACOB'S LADDER

Spiritual

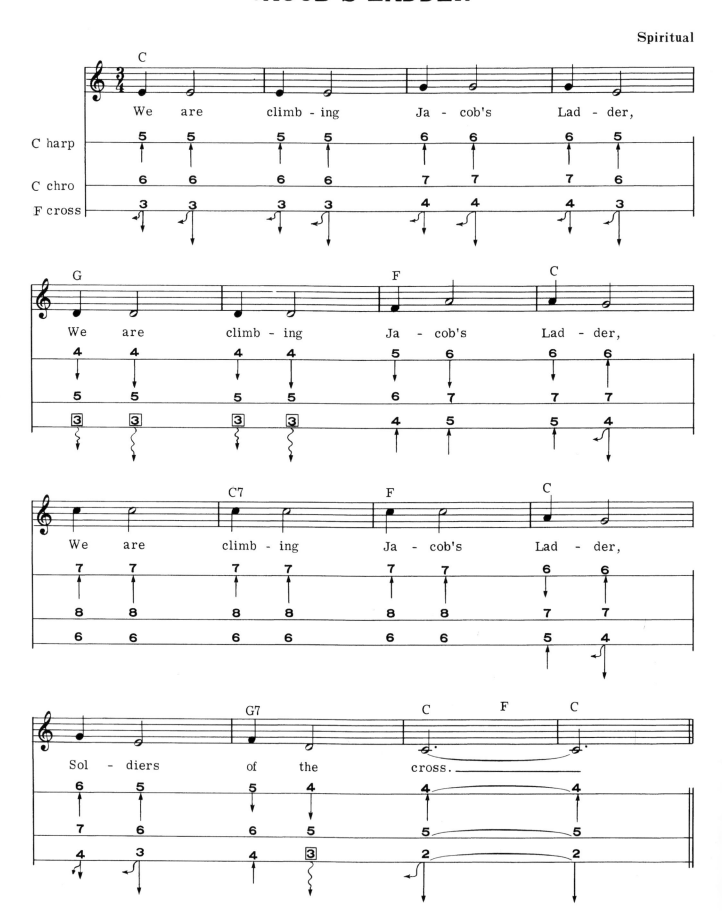

JESUS LOVES ME

William B. Bradbury

I HAVE DECIDED TO FOLLOW JESUS

India Folk Melody

GIVE ME OIL IN MY LAMP

A. Sevison

CHRIST AROSE

Robert Lowry (1826-1899)

BRINGING IN THE SHEAVES

Knowles Shaw (1834-1878)

George A. Minor (1845-1904)

BLESSED ASSURANCE

Fanny Crosby (1820-1915)

Phoebe Knapp (1839-1908)

BENEATH THE CROSS OF JESUS

E. C. Clephane (1830-1869)   F. C. Maker (1844-1927)

SILENT NIGHT

Joseph Mohr (1792-1848)   Franz Gruber (1787-1863)

JOY TO THE WORLD

Isaac Watts (1674-1748)

G. F. Handel (1685-1759)

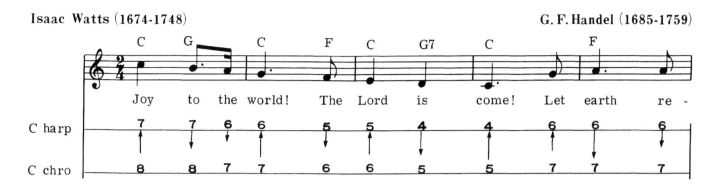

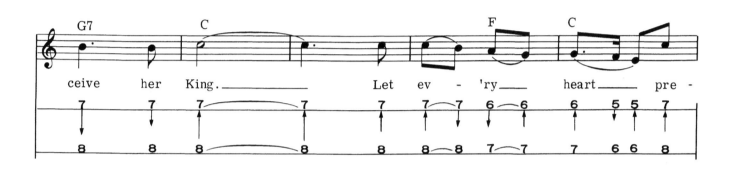

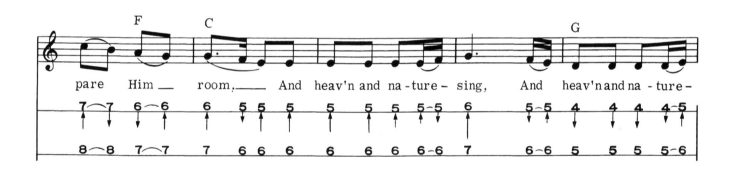

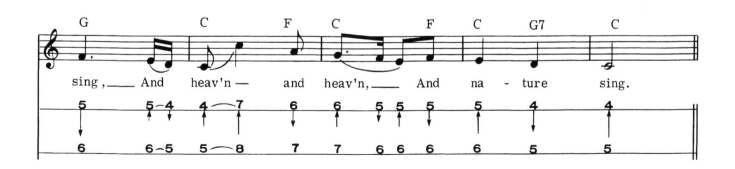

For I Am Not Ashamed Of The Gospel Of Christ . . . Romans 1:16

G harmonica, Diatonic

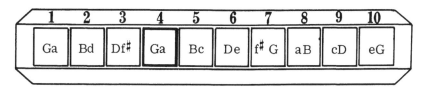

1	2	3	4	5	6	7	8	9	10
Ga	Bd	Df#	Ga	Bc	De	f# G	aB	cD	eG

C Cross - Harp

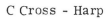

1	2	3	4	5	6	7	8	9	10
Cd	Eg	Gb	Cd	Ef	Ga	bC	dE	fG	aC

(Harp in C)

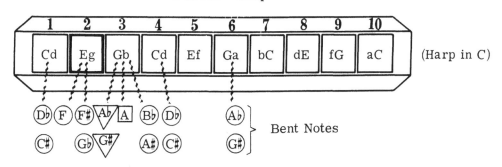

Bent Notes

C harmonica, Chromatic

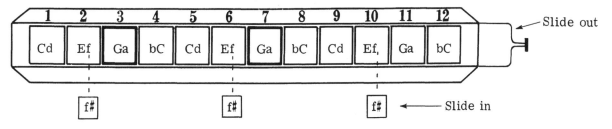

1	2	3	4	5	6	7	8	9	10	11	12
Cd	Ef	Ga	bC	Cd	Ef	Ga	bC	Cd	Ef,	Ga	bC

Slide out

Slide in

KEY OF G
COME AND GO WITH ME
(TO MY FATHERS HOUSE)

HE IS LORD

JESUS BREAKS EVERY FETTER

Composer Unknown

ONLY TRUST HIM

John H. Stockton (1813-1877)

PRAISE HIM IN THE MORNING

JESUS LOVES THE LITTLE CHILDREN

George F. Root (1820-1895)

MUST JESUS BEAR THE CROSS ALONE?

Thomas Shepherd (1665-1739)   George N. Allen (1812-1877)

OLD ONE HUNDREDTH

Thomas Ken (1637-1711)   Louis Bourgeois (c. 1510-1561)

WONDERFUL WORDS OF LIFE

P. P. Bliss (1838-1876)

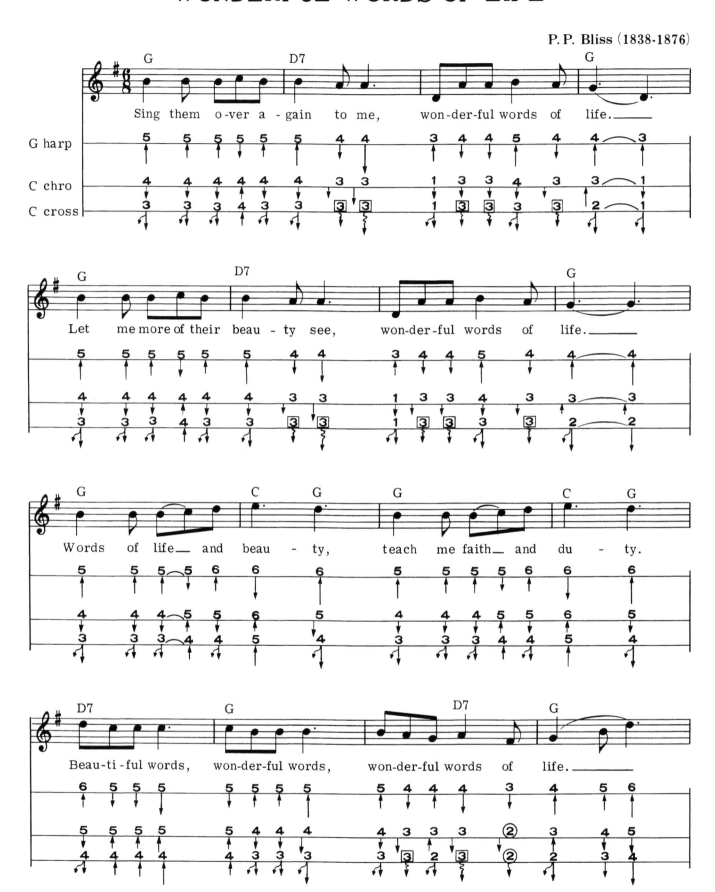

TAKE THIS OLD WORLD

Composer Unknown

WONDERFUL PEACE

W. D. Cornell 19th Century

W. G. Cooper 19th Century

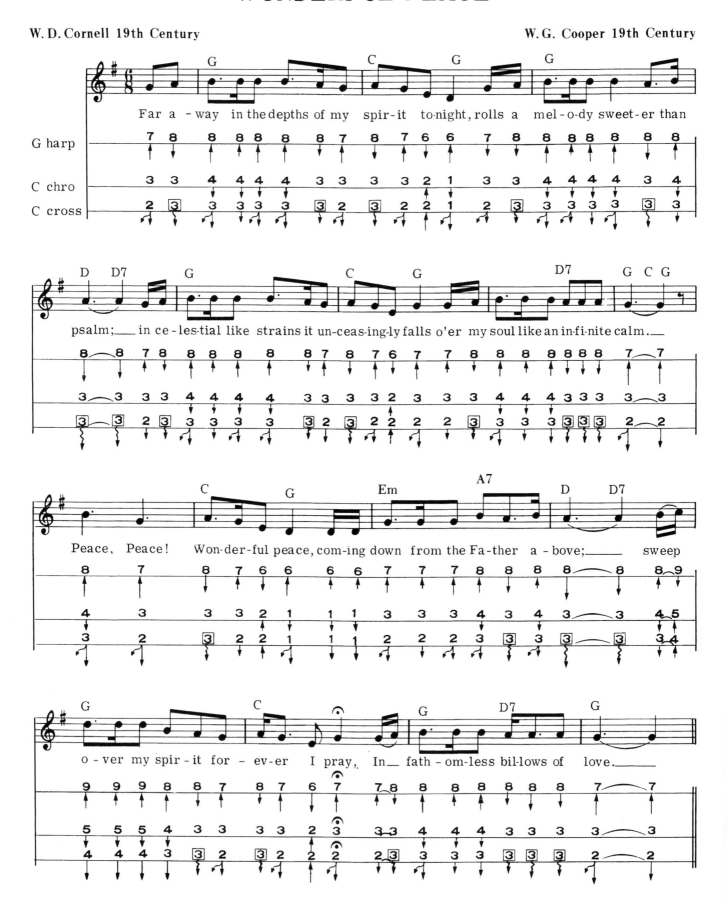

WHAT THE WORLD NEEDS IS JESUS

Ben A. Baur   Ben A. Baur

It is a good thing to give thanks unto the Lord ... upon an instrument... with a solemn sound. Psalm 92:1—3

TO GOD BE THE GLORY

Fanny Crosby (1820-1915)

William H. Doune (1832-1915)

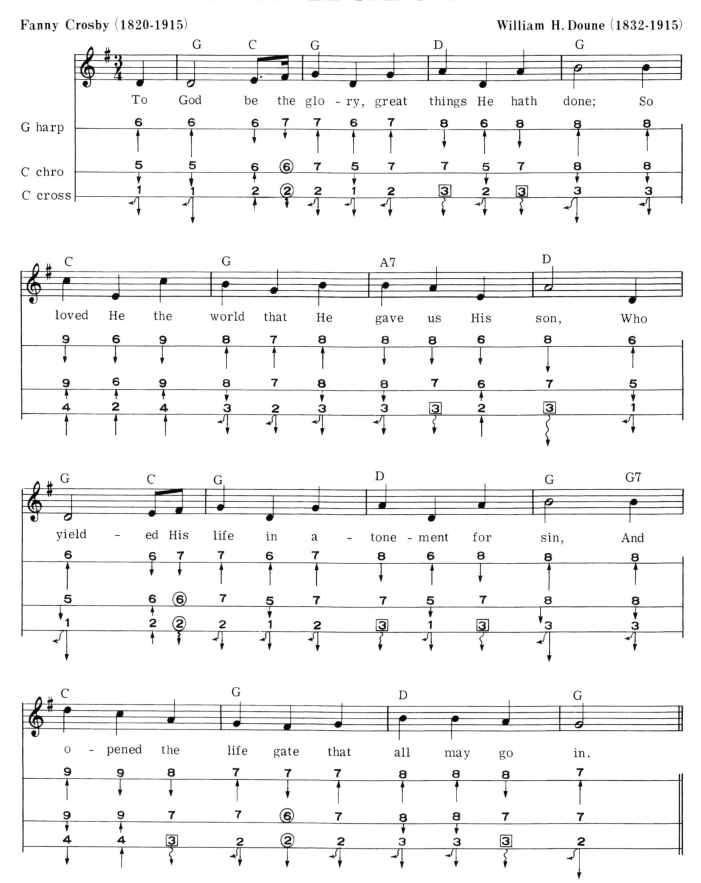

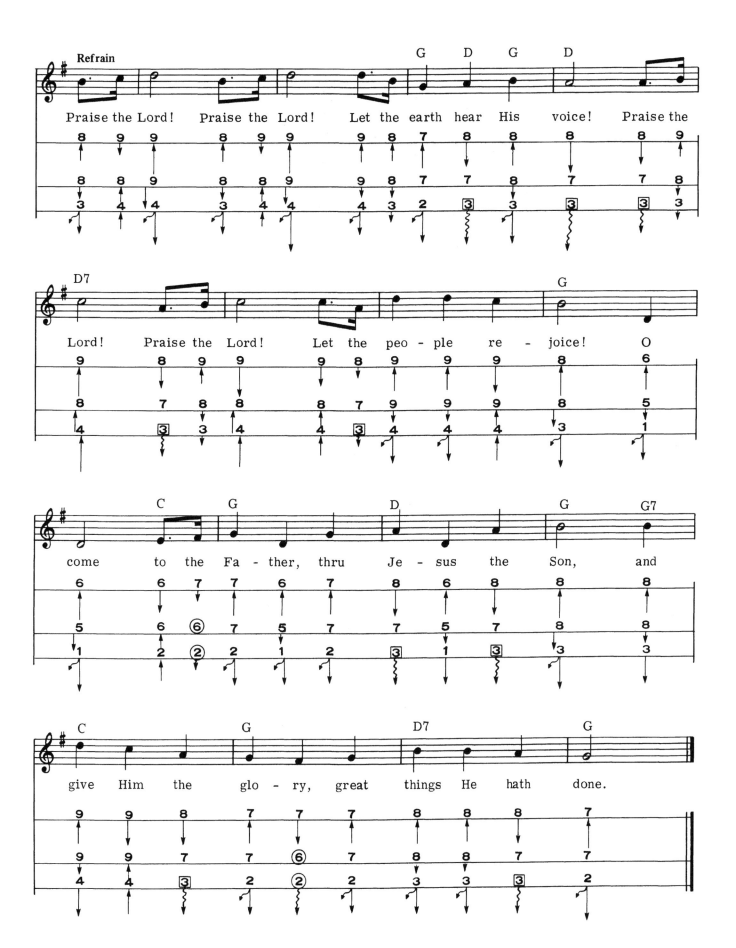

WHAT CHILD IS THIS ?

William C. Dix (1837-1898)

Old English Melody

42

TIS SO SWEET

Louisa M. R. Stead (1850-1917) William J. Kirkpatrick (1838-1921)

43

TAKE MY LIFE AND LET IT BE

Frances R. Havergal (1836-1879) H. A. Cesar Malan (1787-1864)

44

THERE'S A RIVER OF LIFE

L. Cusebolt

THE HALLELUJAH SIDE

Johnson Oatman, Jr. (1856-1922)

J. Howard Entwisle

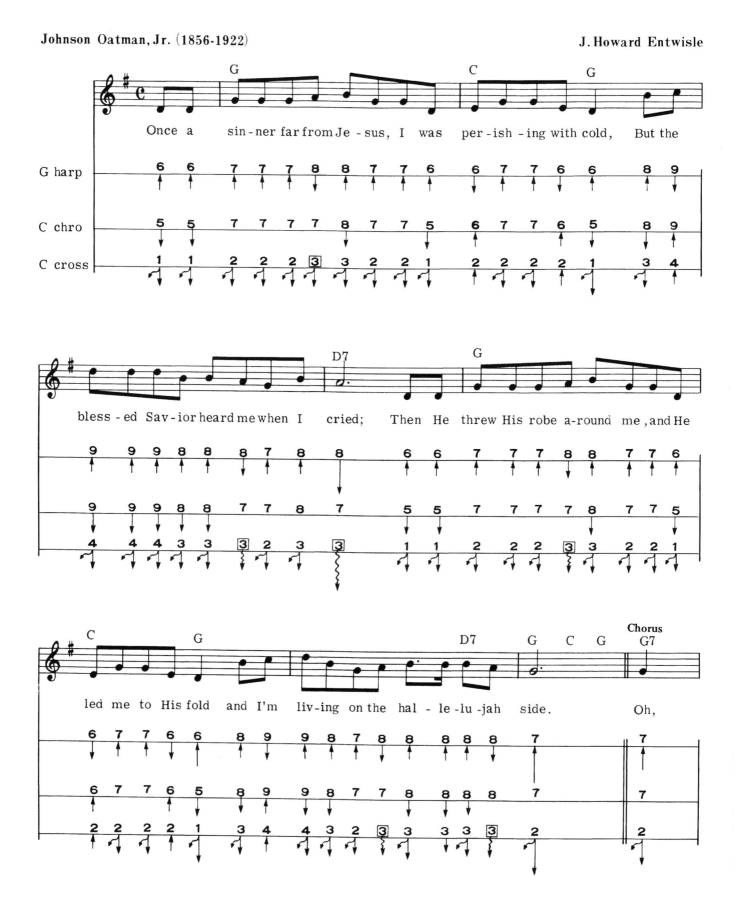

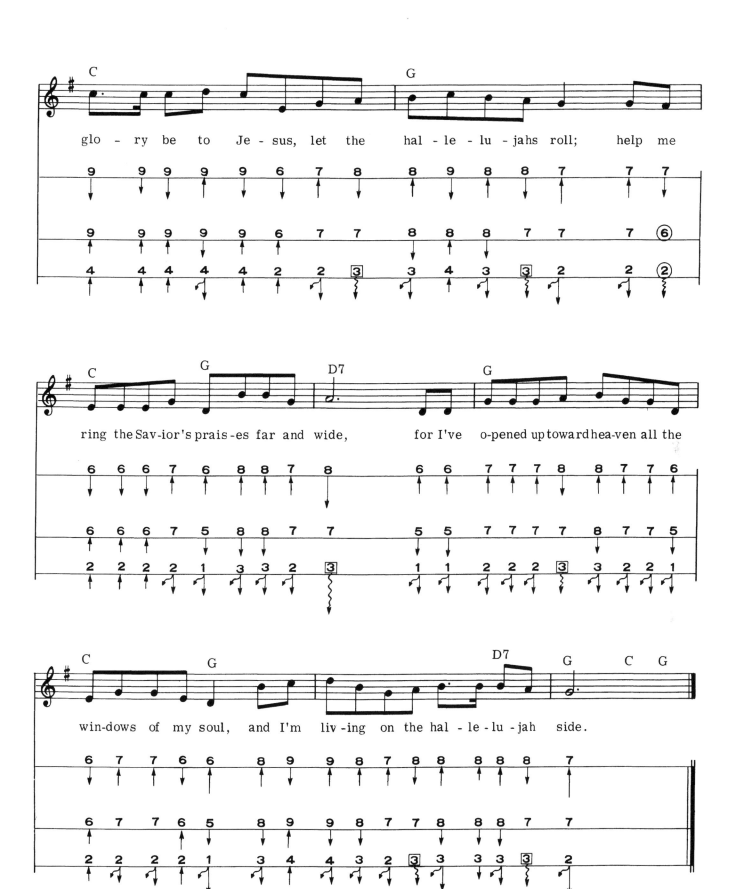

STAND UP, STAND UP FOR JESUS

George Duffield, Jr. (1818-1888)

George J. Webb (1803-1887)

ROCK OF AGES

Angust M. Toplady (1740-1778)   Thomas Hastings (1782-1872)

Let everything that has breath praise the Lord. Psalm 150:6

PRAISE HIM ! PRAISE HIM!

Fanny J. Crosby (1820-1915)   Chester G. Allen (1838-1878)

Praise Him! praise Him! Je-sus our blessed Re-deem-er!

Sing, O Earth, His won-der-ful love pro-claim! Hail Him!

Hail Him! High-est arch-an-gels in glo-ry; strength and hon-or

50

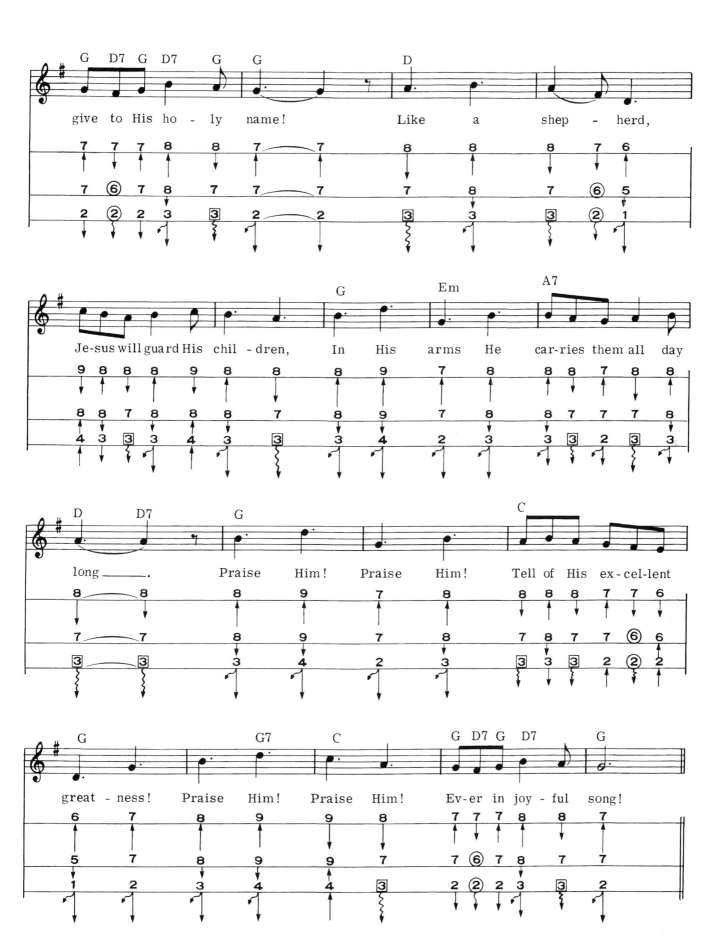

PRECIOUS MEMORIES

J. B. F. Wright

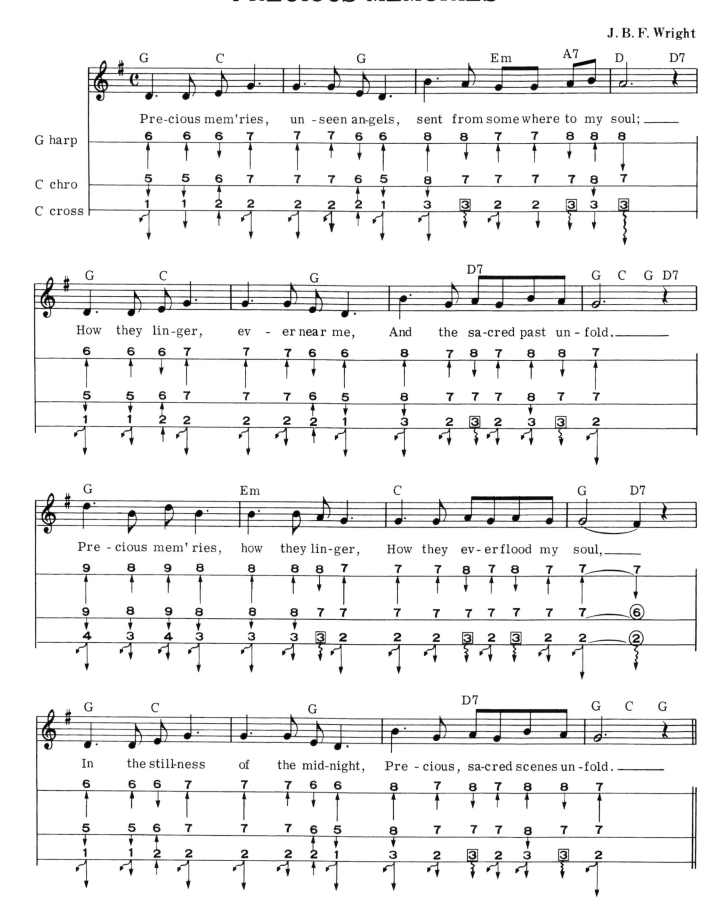

POWER IN THE BLOOD

Lewis E. Jones (1865-1936)

Would you be free from your bur-den of sin? There's pow'r in the blood, pow'r in the blood;

G harp	6	6	6	6	6	6	6	6	6	6	7	7	8	8	8	7	8	8	8
C chro	5	5	5	5	5	5	6	6	6	5	7	⑥	7	7	7	7	8	8	8
C cross	1	1	1	1	1	1	2	2	2	1	2	②	③	③	③	2	3	3	3

Would you o'er e-vil a vic-to-ry win? There's won-der-ful pow'r in the blood.

	6	6	6	6	6	6	6	6	6	6	7	7	7	7	8	7	7	7
	5	5	5	5	5	5	6	6	6	5	7	⑥	⑥	7	7	7	⑥	7
	1	1	1	1	1	1	2	2	2	1	2	②	②	2	③	2	②	2

Chorus

There is pow'r, pow'r, won-der work-ing pow'r, in the blood, of the Lamb. There is

	6	7	8	8	8	7	7	6	6	7	7	7	8	8	6	7
	5	7	8	8	7	7	7	6	5	⑥	7	7	7	8	5	7
	1	2	3	3	③	2	2	2	1	②	2	③	2	③	3	1	2

pow'r, pow'r, won-der work-ing pow'r, in the pre-cious blood of the Lamb!

	8	8	8	7	7	6	6	7	7	8	9	8	8	8	7
	8	8	7	7	7	6	5	⑥	7	7	8	8	7	7	7
	3	3	③	2	2	2	1	②	2	③	4	3	③	③	2

53

PEACE I GIVE YOU

Bill Bay

PASS ME NOT

Fanny J. Crosby (1820-1915)

William H. Doune (1832-1915)

O COME ALL YE FAITHFUL

Trans. by Frederick Oakeley
(1862-1880)

From Wade's Cantus Diversi,
1751

NOTHING BUT THE BLOOD

Robert Lowry (1826-1899)

LEANING ON THE EVERLASTING ARMS

Elisha A. Hoffman (1839-1929)

Anthony J. Showalter

JUST A CLOSER WALK

Source Unknown

I NEED THEE EVERY HOUR

Annie S. Hawks (1835-1918)　　　　　　　　　　　　　　　　　Robert Lowry (1826-1899)

I AM THINE, O LORD

Fanny J. Crosby (1820-1915)   William H. Doane (1832-1915)

I will praise Thee, O Lord, my God, with all my heart. Psalm 86:12

HEAVENLY FATHER, WE APPRECIATE YOU

Source Unknown

HEAVEN, HEAVEN

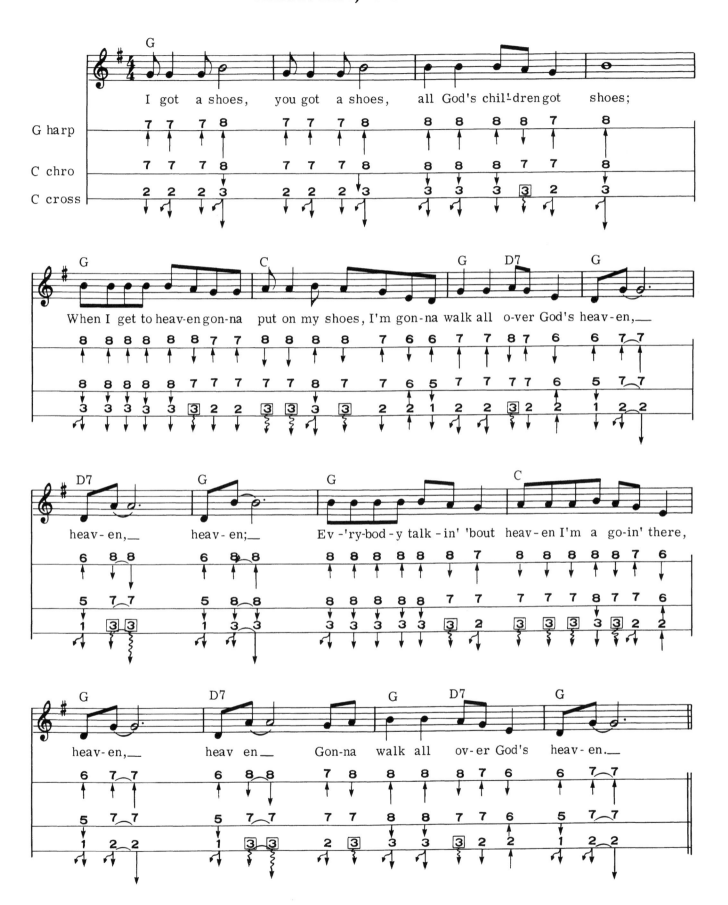

DO, LORD

Spiritual

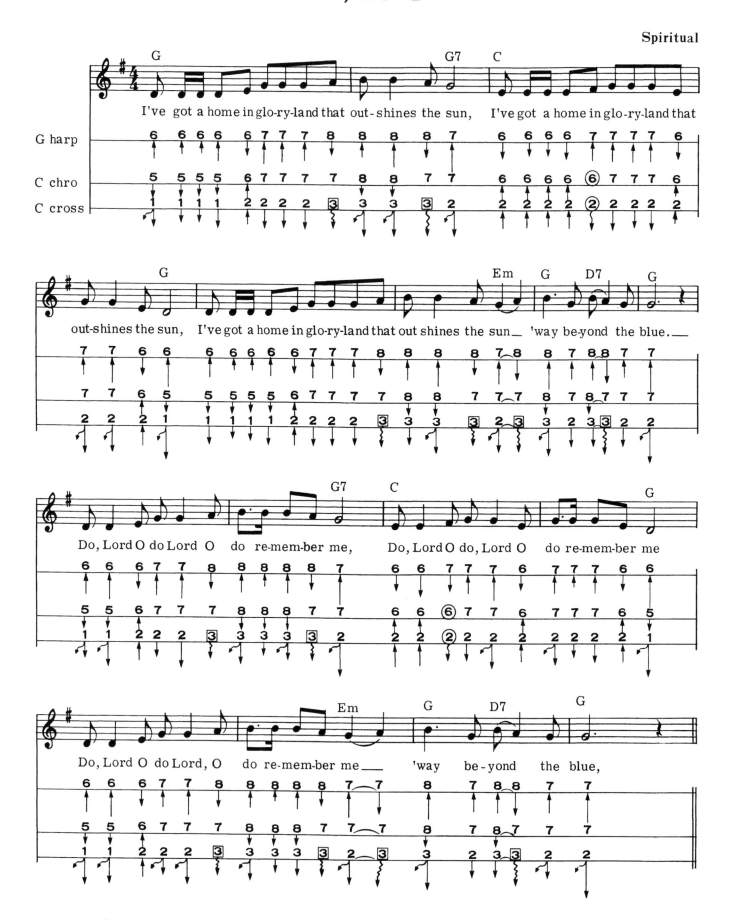

64

COME AND GO WITH ME

Spiritual

CLOSE TO THEE

Fanny J. Crosby (1820-1915)

Silas J. Vail (1818-1884)

BLESSED QUIETNESS

Marie P. Ferguson 19th Century

W. S. Marshell 19th Century

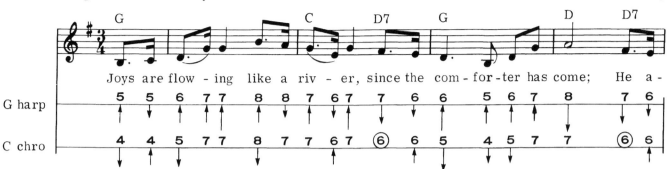

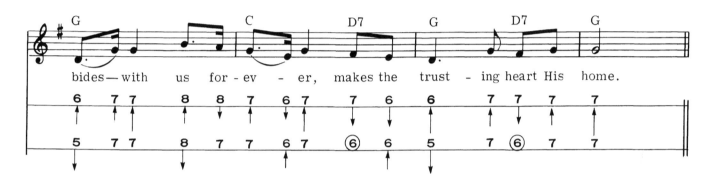

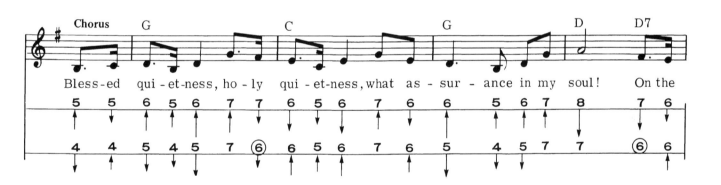

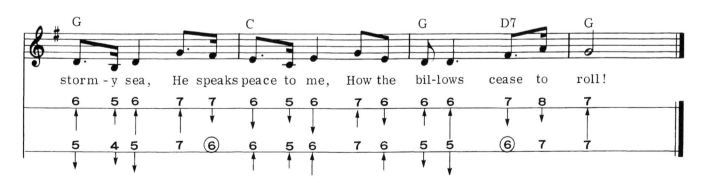

BLESSED BE THE NAME

Charles Wesley (1707-1788)

Ralph E. Hudson (1843-1901)

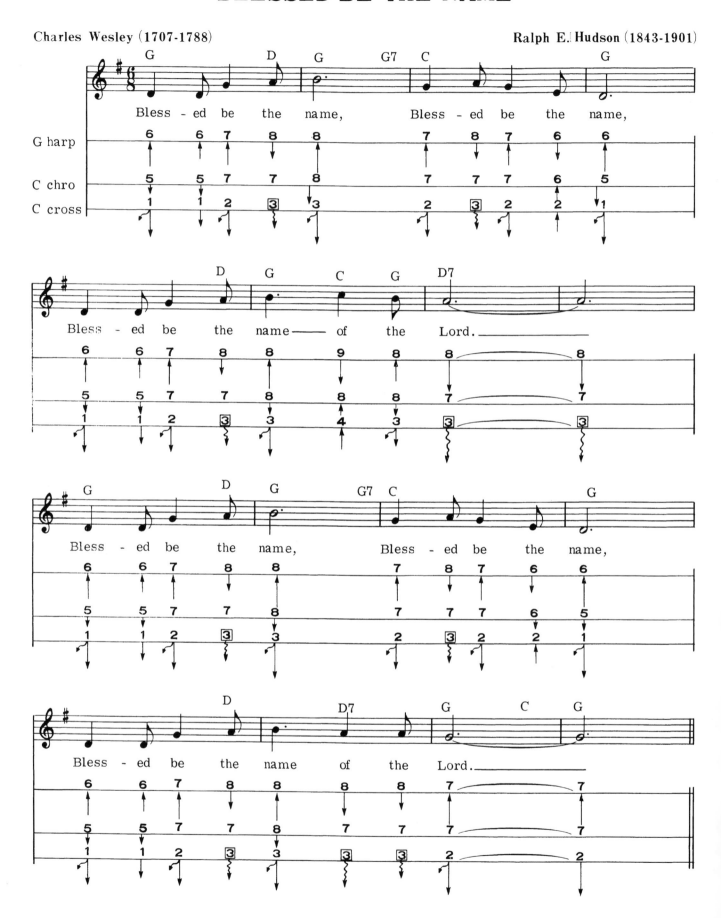

BALM IN GILEAD

Spiritual

AMAZING GRACE

John Newton (1725-1807)

Early American Melody

ALMOST PERSUADED

Philip P. Bliss (1838-1876)

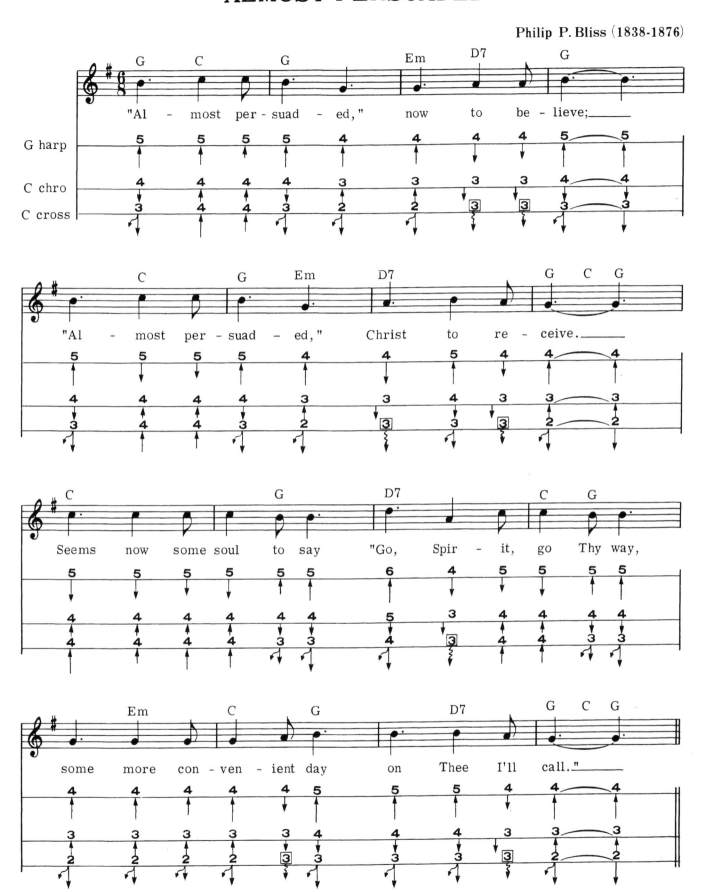

SWEET BY AND BY

S. F. Bennett   J. P. Webster

Rejoice In the Lord Always: And Again I Say Rejoice. Phil. 4:4

I can do all things through Christ which strengtheneth me. Phil.4:13

D harmonica, Diatonic

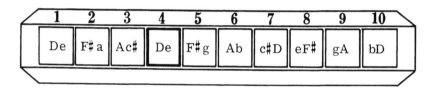

G Cross - Harp

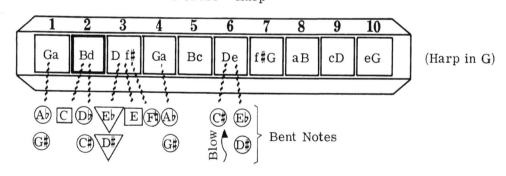

(Harp in G)

C harmonica, Chromatic

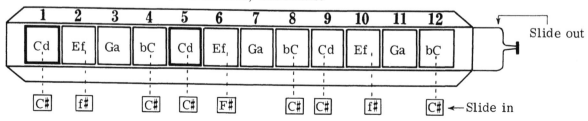

KEY OF D
GOD IS SO GOOD

African Christian Folk Song

JESUS IS THE SWEETEST NAME I KNOW

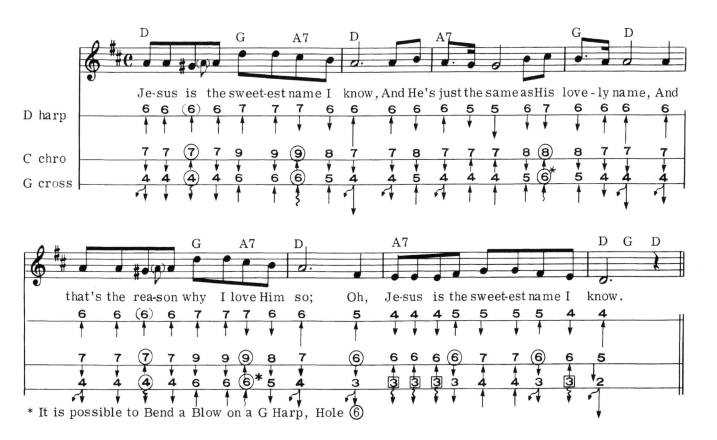

* It is possible to Bend a Blow on a G Harp, Hole ⑥

SHALL WE GATHER AT THE RIVER?

Robert Lowry (1826-1899)

ONWARD CHRISTIAN SOLDIERS

Sobine Baring-Gould (1834-1924)

A. S. Sullivan (1842-1900)

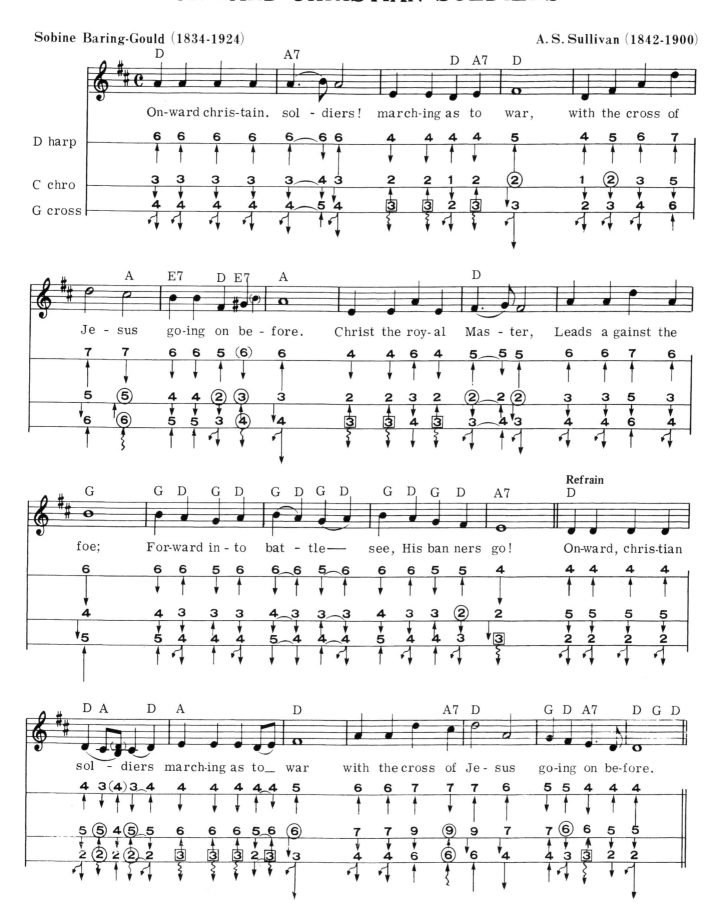

ON JORDAN'S STORMY BANKS

Samuel Stemett (1727-1795)

American Folk Melody

MY FAITH LOOKS UP TO THEE

Ray Palmer (1808-1887)

Lowell Mason (1792-1872)

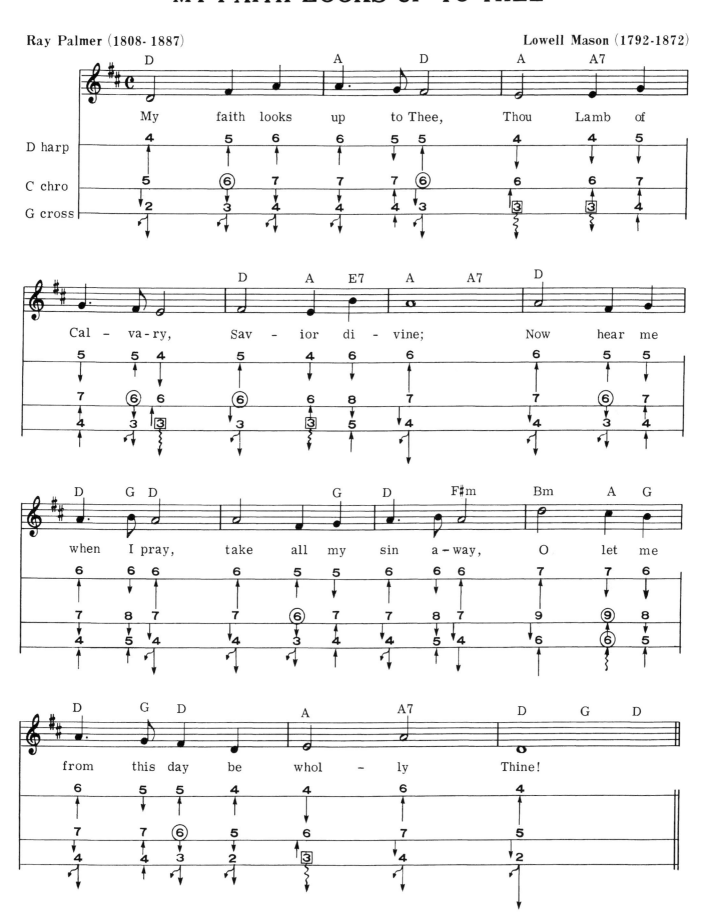

LORD, I WANT TO BE A CHRISTIAN

Spiritual

LET US BREAK BREAD TOGETHER

American Folk Hymn

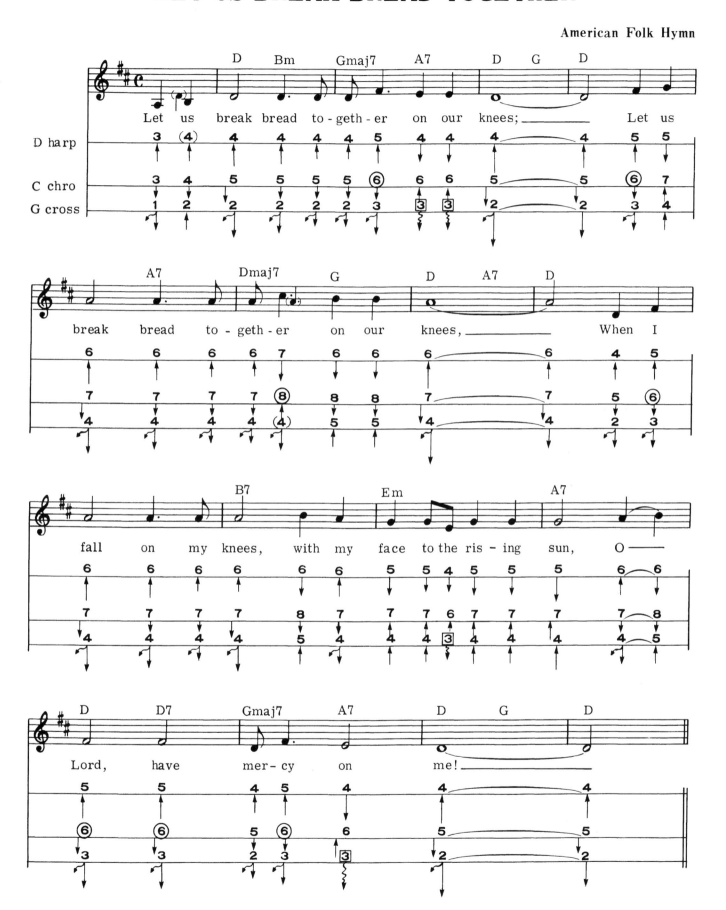

When a man's ways please the Lord, he maketh even his enemies to be at peace with him. Proverbs 16:7

I WILL PRAISE HIM

Margaret J. Harris 19th Century

JUST AS I AM

Charlotte Elliott (1789-1871)   William Bradbury (1816-1868)

FAIREST LORD JESUS

Adapted by Richard S. Willis
(1819-1900)

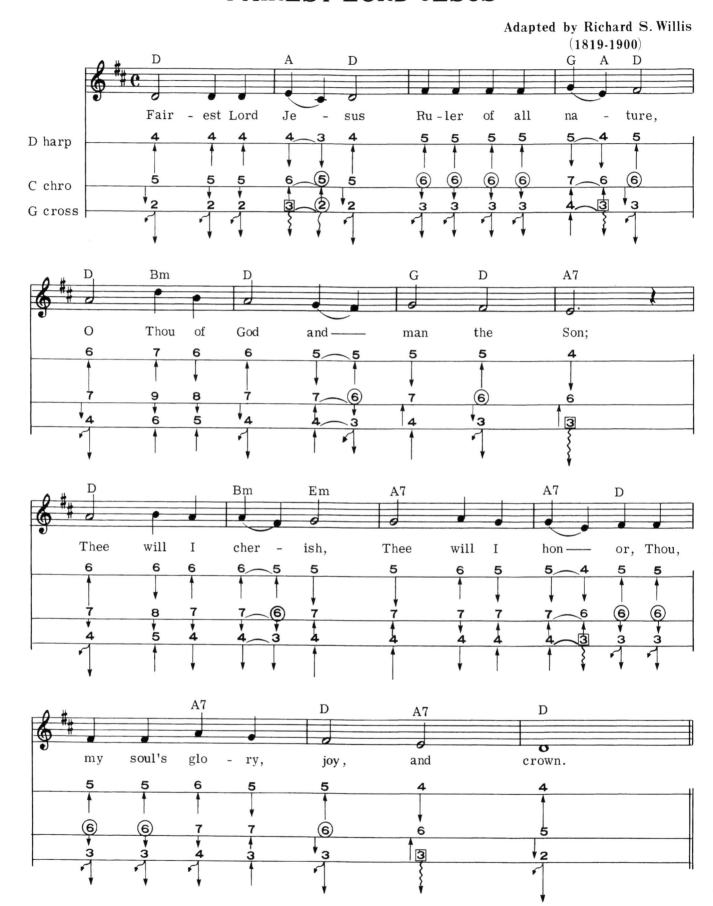

AT THE CROSS

Isaac Watts (1674-1748)
Chorus: R. E. Hudson

Ralph E. Hudson (1843-1901)

ABIDE WITH ME

Henry Lyte (1793-1847)   William H. Monk (1883-1889)

That Ye Might Walk Worthy of the Lord Unto All Pleasing, Being Fruitful In Every Good Work, And Increasing In The Knowledge Of God. Colossians 1:10

Let the word of Christ dwell in you in all wisdom; teaching and admonishing one another in Psalms and Hymns and spiritual songs... Colossians 3:16

F harmonica, Diatonic

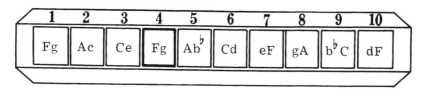

Bb Cross - Harp

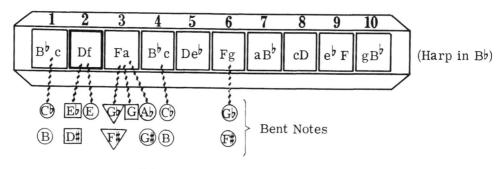

C harmonica, Chromatic

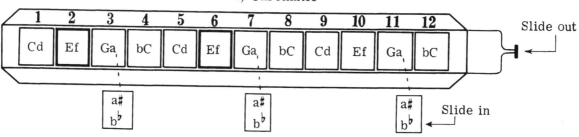

KEY OF F
WHISPER A PRAYER

Composer Unknown

WHERE HE LEADS ME

E. W. Brandy 19th Century

John S. Norris (1844-1907)

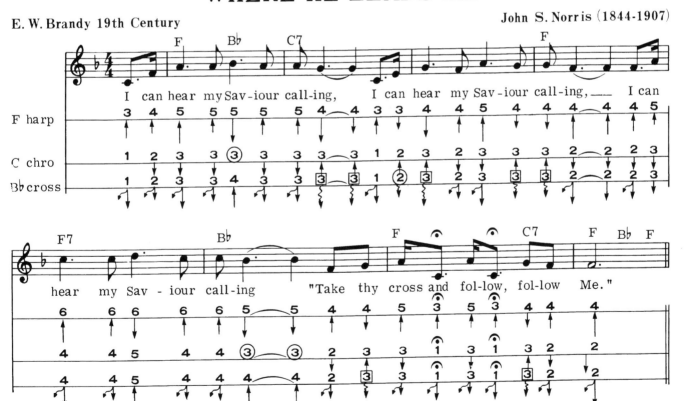

Because of the High Pitch, F Diatonic Harp will be notated in Holes 2-7.

LONESOME VALLEY

Spiritual

PEACE LIKE A RIVER

WHEN I SURVEY THE WONDROUS CROSS

Isaac Watts (1674-1748)

Gregorian Chant

WHAT A FRIEND WE HAVE IN JESUS

Joseph Scriven (1820-1886)

Charles C. Converse (1832-1918)

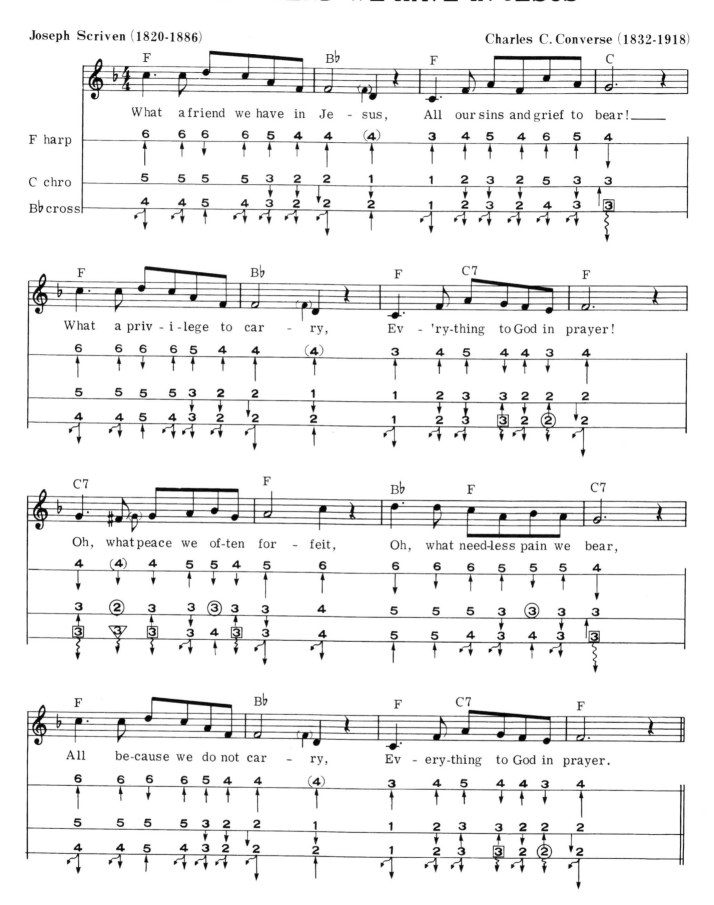

WERE YOU THERE

Spiritual

TO BE LIKE JESUS

Composer Unknown

THIS IS THE DAY

Composer Unknown

SWING LOW, SWEET CHARIOT

* C harp is used to play this song, because it does not require a B♭ tone.

Spiritual

REVIVE US AGAIN

Wiliam P. Mackay (1839-1885)

J. J. Husband (1760-1825)

CAUSE ME TO COME

OH, THE BLOOD OF JESUS

Source Unknown

O HOW I LOVE JESUS

Frederick Whitfield (1829-1904)

American Melody

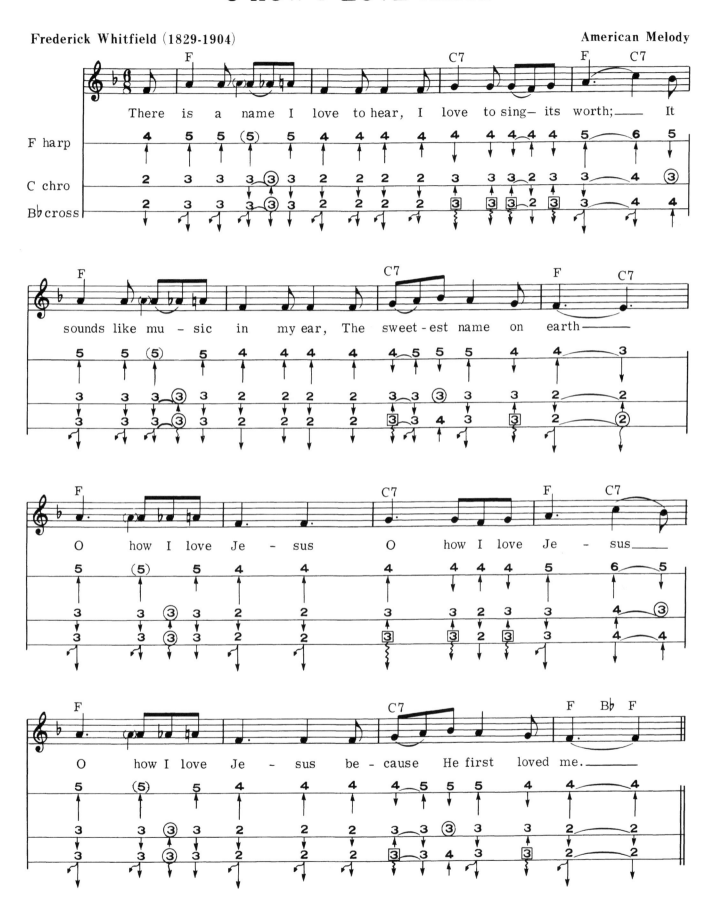

NEAR THE CROSS

Fanny J. Crosby (1820-1915)

William H. Doune (1832-1915)

GREAT IS THE LORD

Psalm 48

Robert Ewing

I'M IN THE LORD'S ARMY

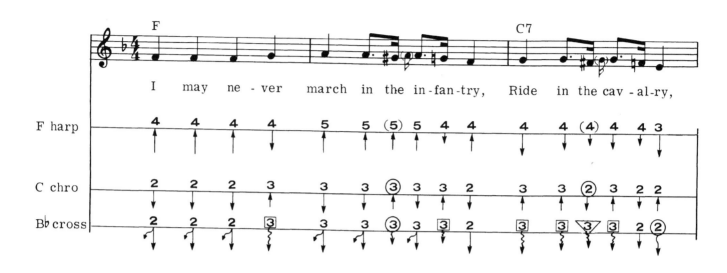

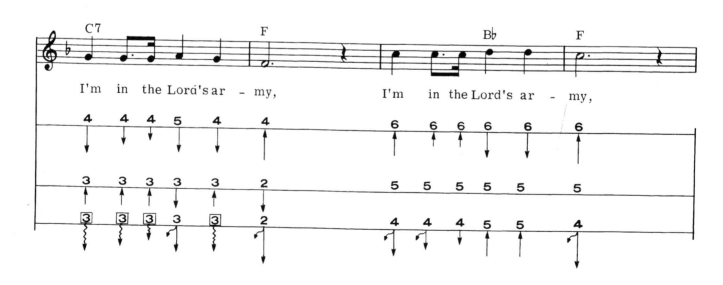

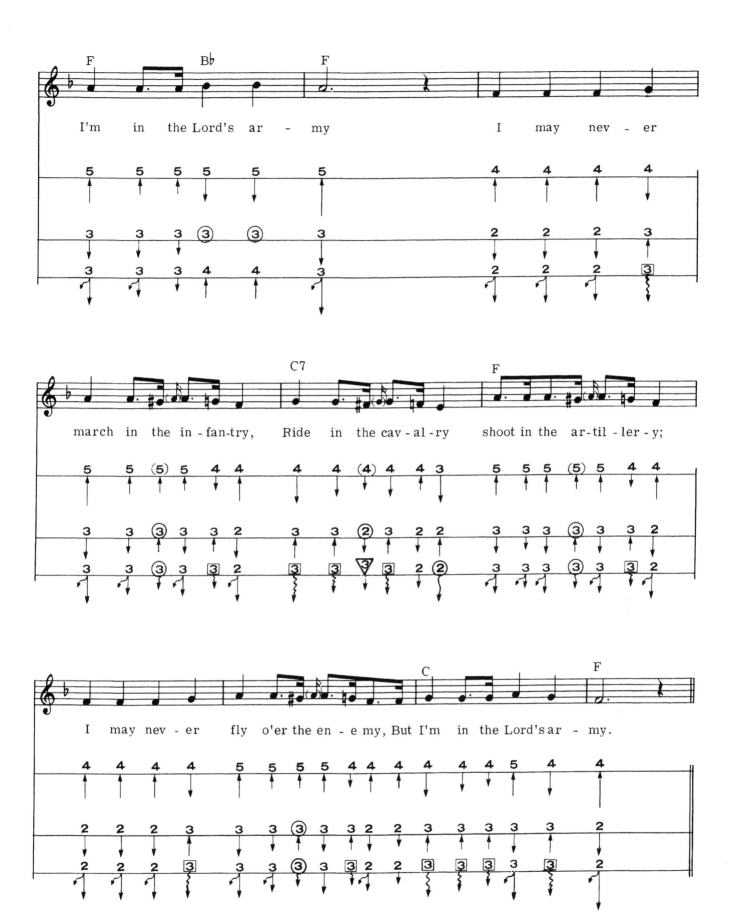

AWAY IN A MANGER

James R. Murray (1841-1905)

GO TELL IT ON THE MOUNTAIN

Spiritual

MY JESUS, I LOVE THEE

William R. Featherston (1846-1873)   Adoniram J. Gordon (1836-1895)

THE SOLID ROCK

Edward Mote (1797-1874)   William B. Bradbury (1816-1868)

109

Make A Joyful Noise Unto The Lord, All Ye Lands. Psalm 100:1

To Everything There Is A Season, And A Time To Every Purpose Under The Heaven. Ecc. 3:1

Great Music at Your Fingertips